11/19/13

QR CODES
KILL KITTENS

QR CODES KILL KITTENS

How to Alienate Customers, Dishearten Employees, and Drive Your Business into the Ground

SCOTT STRATTEN

WILEY

Published by John Wiley & Sons, Inc., Hoboken, New Jersey.
Published simultaneously in Canada.

For general information about our other products and services, please contact our Customer Care Department within the United States at (800) 762-2974, outside the United States at (317) 572-3993 or fax (317) 572-4002.

Wiley publishes in a variety of print and electronic formats and by print-on-demand. Some material included with standard print versions of this book may not be included in e-books or in print-on-demand. If this book refers to media such as a CD or DVD that is not included in the version you purchased, you may download this material at http://booksupport.wiley.com. For more information about Wiley products, visit www.wiley.com.

Library of Congress Cataloging-in-Publication Data:
  Stratten, Scott–
  QR Codes Kill Kittens: How to Alienate Customers, Dishearten Employees, and Drive Your Business into the Ground/Scott Stratten.
     pages cm.
  ISBN: 978-1-118-73275-5 (cloth); ISBN: 978-1-118-78687-1 (ebk);
  ISBN: 978-1-118-78690-1 (ebk)
  1. QR codes. 2. Management. 3. Marketing. 4. Information technology—Management. I. Title.
  HF5416.S77 2014
  658—dc23

                                                                2013022153

Printed in the United States of America

10 9 8 7 6 5 4 3 2 1

Introduction

Friends, followers, countrymen, lend me your ears.

I come to praise QR codes, not to bury them.

QR codes are full of potential. The thing is, we're breaking them—before we even get a chance to figure out just how awesome they can be.

Every time you use a QR code for your business because you can, and not because you should, whether your market wants them or not, a kitten dies—a sweet, innocent kitten.

QR codes are the perfect example of a bright and shiny business tool. We see them, and they are quite simply too exciting to ignore.

In case you've picked up this book without knowing what a QR code is, let me run it down for you. A QR code is a kind of bar code (*QR* stands for quick response). To read them, you need to have a smartphone and download a QR code–reading app. Once on your phone, the app will allow you to, in theory, scan the code. If the app works, the code was made correctly, and if you are able to hold your phone steadily over the code for long enough, you will be taken to a website, download link, or destination that is mobile-friendly and therefore easily readable on your phone.

Mobile technology at its best, right?

Wrong.

All of a sudden QR codes are everywhere. We just can't help ourselves. We see QR codes in magazines and on billboards, on bus stops, and on products themselves.

The truth is, QR codes don't usually work. We are using QR codes to show that we're using QR codes.

We ignore the things we should be doing in our businesses to create and place them. We ignore fixing problems. We put aside improving our products, listening to our customers, and cleaning up the tools we are already using. We ignore basic issues of functionality. We yell, "Squirrel!" and run after them.

QR codes take up our valuable time, and space, and let us ignore what we should be fixing and focusing on in business. QR codes are a selfish "Look at me and how tech savvy I am" marketing tool. More often than not, they are just another hoop we make our would-be customers jump through.

A lot of business books out there are going to tell you what you should be doing. Well, this one is a little different.

QR codes alienate customers, dishearten employees, and drive your business into the ground, not to mention kill kittens.

I am going to show you that QR codes represent what's wrong with business today, for four different reasons:

They don't work.

Nobody likes them.

They are selfish.

They take up valuable time better spent elsewhere.

The book is laid out using these four reasons as chapter headings. QR code misuse sets the tone for each of the four sections, and we expand on each reason using examples from throughout business.

He who hath brought many QR codes home to clients, whose return on investment needs they do not fulfill, I speak to you.[1]

Let's do this.

---

[1] Apologies to Mr. Shakespeare.

CHAPTER 1

They Don't Work

They Missed a Step

I don't know where this QR code takes me when scanned. I wish I did. I tried to follow the "three easy steps," but I feel like one important step is missing.

Figure Credit: Thanks for sharing @HaleyCertified; used with permission.

Step 0.5: Don't put QR code behind giant bar.

The code is unscannable. It's taking up valuable space, looking fancy and modern, and doing absolutely nothing.

This is my main issue with QR codes and so many of the things we try in business—they just don't work.

We need to be thinking about functionality for our customers.

Did you know that 50 percent of people who scan a QR code would never scan one again? You know why? Because it didn't work. It didn't bring value. It made people jump through an unnecessary and all-too-often nonfunctioning hoop.

Stop it.

Craptcha

Captchas. Making it impossible to log in since 1997.

Not Working

Kinda like most QR codes, this guy doesn't work either.

When I worked in human resources, I would put ads in the paper for positions requiring three to five years' experience.

Why three to five years?

I honestly have no idea.

The only difference I can see between someone with five years' retail experience and one year is that the person with five years' experience hates people more.

A Kitten Dies . . .

. . . every time someone tweets advice about how to build a massive following—and only has 23 followers.

Anybody Got a Pen?

Anybody got a pen?

Invasion of Sanity and Sanitation

Trying to aim, while trying to aim, is not a good idea.

Figure Credit: Thanks to @GregScott for this awesome; used with permission.

A Kitten Dies . . .

. . . if your idea of successful networking is giving out your cards to 200+ people.

You're doing it wrong. Card connect, not collect. It just won't work.

I Don't Feel Special

Volume discount. You're doing it wrong.

A Kitten Dies . . .

. . . every time someone runs a Facebook contest without thinking. When you give away a free iPad, all you end up with is a whole lot of likes from people who like free iPads.

The Door to Digital Success

Step 1: Put QR code on door.

Step 2: Make the code small enough that people need to get really close to scan it.

Step 3: As they approach, have the door automatically open into the people.

Step 4: Profit!

Twipster

Tweeting to spite themselves and refusing to tweet back.

Hipster Twitter.

Everyone talking and nobody wants to be there.

O Canada

Watch the trailer:

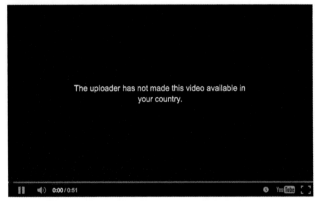

This is what being Canadian on the Internet looks like.

Working Hard

James P
@PenguinShepherd

👤▾   🐦 Follow

The guy watching porn at work across the
road is back, doesn't realise our whole office
can see him! pic.twitter.com/aoOMGJGfYs

↩ Reply   🔁 Retweet   ⭐ Favorite   ••• More

2,594   **537**
RETWEETS   FAVORITES

And you were worried about your employees
being on Facebook all day . . .

Mistaken Mobile Metrics

"Up to 50% of the impressions served on a static mobile banner ad are from accidental clicks or 'fat finger' taps."[1]

---

[1] GoldSpot Media, quoted in "Mobile Advertising's Darkest Secret: Here's the REAL Error Rate for 'Fat Finger' Clicks," Samantha Felix, *Business Insider*, October 26, 2012, http://read.bi/17m8dUm.

Caution! Moving Walkway Ends before You Scan the QR Code!

I've seen people trip on moving walkways, when they aren't even walking on them.

Figure Credit: Thanks @Amadeus_IOM for sharing; used with permission.

The Unknown Icon

Using an icon without an address leaves people to their own Internet skills and intelligence to find you. Never leave people to their own intelligence.

A Kitten Dies . . .

. . . when your app isn't an app.

My bank recently launched an app to much fanfare.

I downloaded it, looking forward to all the ways it would make banking easier and better.

When I opened it, it took me to their website.

Congratulations! You just launched a link.

Where QR Codes Belong

Twenty years ago, QR codes were created for manufacturers. They were better options than bar codes when a lot of information needed to be shared.

They are still used for this purpose in many industries today.

So, if you see a QR code in your toilet, that's exactly where it belongs.

Figure Credit: Thanks to @porknbomb and @craigcaruso for sharing; used with permission.

E.T., Don't Phone Home

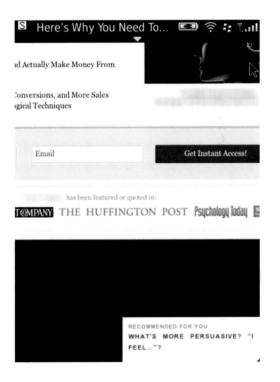

This is what happens when you combine your blog with a pop-up on a mobile phone.

Ta-da! I just left your website.

Going Viral Isn't a Science

"According to pretend scientists, the most retweeted words in history are 'Justin Bieber You Social Media +link+ please RT.'"

"Please add the preceding content into our social-media feeds so we too can go viral."

Listen, you can't make anything go viral, but what I can promise you is if you provide consistent, quality content that is valued by your followers, it will get shared. (For the non–social media geeks, *viral* describes online content that becomes widely popular overnight.)

Pinterest Fail

Objects on Pinterest may be harder to create than they appear.

Phone Call on LAN 2

Social is the new personal phone call.

If your employees spend all their time on Facebook, you don't have a social media problem. You have a hiring problem or a management problem.

The Autofollow

Social media is about whom you connect with, not how many people you connect with.

Following fake accounts makes you look fake, too.

Seems Legit

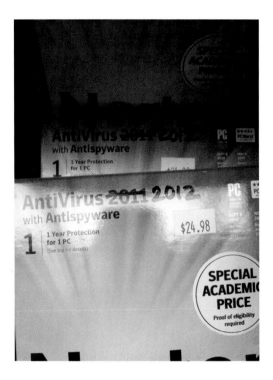

Poor Wendy(s)

1. Invite customers to make something go viral.
2. Put out flyers two weeks before the contest starts.
3. Use an apostrophe in the Twitter handle incorrectly, leading entrants to tweet @Wendy instead of @Wendys.

@Wendy sure did get a lot of mentions that week! The innocent Canadian was unimpressed.

A Kitten Dies . . .

. . . when I once asked someone why it had taken her three months to reply to a tweet of mine in which I'd asked about a product, and she replied, "I've been busy."

Seriously?

Who are you? Gandhi? Are you wandering through a desert with no Wi-Fi that you're too busy to get back to me?

If you really are too busy to reply to a would-be customer, you're too busy for social media. Don't use it.

Tunnel of QR Love

Found in a Toronto subway, far below the reach of Wi-Fi.

Figure Credit: Thanks to @iDanielSaa for this one; used with permission.

Spaced Out

Cody Andrus @candrus68   28 Jan
@unmarketing Have you seen the hashtag for the film Safe Haven? It
has a space in it. In ALL the ads. #SafeHaven or #Safe Haven?
Collapse ← Reply ↻ Retweet ★ Favorite ••• More

Scott Stratten @unmarketing   28 Jan
@candrus68 oh god
Expand

Figure Credit: Thanks to @candrus68 for sharing; used with permission.

A Kitten Dies . . .

. . . when companies put zero tolerance firing policies in place.

Unless you plan on firing someone for taking a Post-it Note, they don't work.

Make sure you aren't losing good employees and making more room for the bad ones.

A BlackBerry by Any Other Name

In early 2013, BlackBerry announced they were changing their name to BlackBerry, from the lesser-known RIM. This was their lead announcement for all the exciting things ahead for the company.

As a lifelong BlackBerry customer, I couldn't be happier with my new iPhone.

Desktop Friendly

Sorry, this website has not been developed for mobile phones or tablets. For the best user experience, please view this site on a desktop computer.

Translation: we neither want to spend the money, nor the time, bringing our website up to 2010 standards. For the only user experience go find a desktop in the library.

What the Truck?

Motion + Dirt + Distance + Lift Gate Obstructing QR code
= an entire breed of cat destroyed.

Swipe Away

Five seconds before this picture was taken in the back of a Las Vegas cab, Steve Wynn came on the screen and told me, "Swipe your phone over the QR code."

I'm not sure which is worse: the fact that it is impossible to get your phone out and to scan before the code disappears or the word *swipe*.

Poor Baby

King Baby Studio
@kingbabystudio

You follow us on twitter right?
fb.me/25Q6ZqW1t

2013-05-04 5:47 PM

1 FAVORITE

Love their style and accessories; hate their synching of social accounts. (For the non–social media geeks, this is a tweet that is a copy of a Facebook status. It makes no sense on Twitter. It's like asking someone in your living room if they've ever seen your house.)

A Kitten Dies . . .

. . . for every dormant social media account.

It's better not to have an account at all than to have a dormant one.

It's like having a storefront that's always locked and a phone that's never answered. It simply doesn't work.

Capital Offense

Susan Boyle Susan will be answering your questions at her exclusive album listening
party on Saturday. Send in your questions #susanalbumparty Susan HQ
30 Oct on Twitter

Using capitals in your hashtags can make the difference between promoting an AlbumParty and your analbumparty . . .

A Kitten Dies . . .

. . . every time someone says he or she is going to make a viral video.

No one makes a video viral.

Viral is a result of awesome content.

Appealing QR Codes

I once saw a QR code on a banana that when scanned took me to a video that was "not playable on a mobile device."

The only things scanning QR codes are mobile devices.

No one is lifting up his or her PC to scan your banana.

A Kitten Dies . . .

. . . any time someone asks to have an original faxed over, not a copy.

I Don't Even . . .

Useless Disclaimer

Confidential: This communication and any attachment(s) may contain confidential or privileged information and is intended solely for the address(es) or the entity representing the recipient(s). If you have received this information in error, you are hereby advised to destroy the document and any attachment(s), make no copies of the same, and inform the sender immediately of the error. Any unauthorized use or disclosure of this information is strictly prohibited.

*   *   *

Seriously. How do you destroy an e-mail?

The total number of lawsuits that have been avoided because of this e-mail disclaimer is zero.

Seriously. Look it up.

Wait, What?

Twenty-four-hour protection. You're doing it wrong.

One Potato, Two Potato, Three Potato, Scan!

Scanning the potato QR code on the left brought me to the nonworking page on the right.

It's almost as effective as pressing the Facebook icon printed underneath it with your finger.

CHAPTER 2

Nobody Likes Them
Not Even Your Lost Pet

Nobody likes QR codes.

Unless you sell them to your clients, unless you just paid to have one added to your copy, unless you just downloaded a code reader and still haven't figured out just how frustrating they are—nobody likes them.

And nobody likes you using them. Not even your lost pet.

The product above is a QR code pet tag designed to help you find your lost pet.

The tag, when scanned, takes you to contact information for your lost dog or cat. At first glance, that seems like a good idea, right? We all want to make sure our precious lost pug or psycho cat is found. (Seriously, there are about 80 known breeds of cats, and this is the one they chose? The hairless cat of Satan?)

Let me break this down for you.

- Eighty-five percent of people have a cell phone.
- Fifty percent of phones are capable of scanning a QR code.
- Seventeen percent of people have scanned a QR code.
- Fifty percent were successful and would scan a QR code again.

This means that 3.6 percent of people scan QR codes.

Ninety-nine percent of people can call a phone number with their phone (1 percent variance).

How about we try something else on the tag? Like a phone number.

No one ever looked at a 10-digit phone number and didn't know what to do with it.

I understand that for this company the cost and scalability of a call center versus that of a website is a huge issue. But if next to no one scans QR codes, then even less than no one will find your lost pet by scanning its neck.

This section is all about the things we hate that businesses do.

A Kitten Dies . . .

. . . every time you send someone a two-line e-mail.

With a 15-line signature.

Scott Stratten
Phone: 1-888-580-9969
E-mail: Scott@unmarketing.com
Twitter: www.twitter.com/unmarketing
Facebook: https://www.facebook.com/
UnMarketing
LinkedIn: http://www.linkedin.com/in/
unmarketing
Pinterest: http://pinterest.com/
unmarketing/
YouTube: http://www.youtube.com/
user/stratola
Instagram: http://instagram.com/
unmarketing
Google+: https://plus.google.com/u/0/
102469951620293509326/posts
MySpace: http://www.myspace.com/
stratola
"inspirational quote"
QR code to another contact page

Making It Rain

I have two pieces of advice for companies that still want to put flyers on windshields:

1. Don't do it in the rain.
2. Don't do it at all.

Well, That's One Way to Reply

 ▶ **Maggie Rita's**
Thursday at 6:18 PM in Houston, Texas · ↩

Happy to see that your location on Shepherd closed! Insulting Houston before we tried your food was kinda "dee-de-deee" of you! We hope they all close soon.

Maggie Rita's
I thought fat people were suppose to be jolly!
Yesterday at 9:59 PM · Like

Putting Your Foot Down on Fonts

Oh, I Know

Robert

It's not who you know....it's who you know, KNOWS! ;)
– Robert

'Share'

Like · Comment · Share · 2 minutes ago · 🌐

I cannot overstate the amount of useless motivational quotes on social media. This one, however, may take the cake. Not only is it a useless quote, but also the person quoted himself and put "Share" afterward. Obviously he saw somewhere that if you ask people to share, they are more likely to. It hurts . . .

BCC Is the New ABC

FW: Marketing, Business Opportunity.

Sent: Wed 08/05/2013 9:42 PM
To: Scott Stratten

From: pro
Date: Wed, 8 May 2013 19:40:36 -0400
To:
<ma
<ds
<an
<ch
<bri
<jer
<ap
<inf
<jth
<ba
<sal
<be

This. Don't do this.

It isn't just the spamming people that's the problem but also putting all the e-mails in the To: line.

There were more than 500 recipients in this e-mail. And guess what everyone did to ask them to stop spamming?

Yup. They replied all.

Social SEO

Google+/-

Justifying Google+ as an incredible social media site because of its SEO value is like going to a networking event and speaking only in keywords.

The Secret to Making You're Book or Blog Go Viral

Just misspell something.

Figure Credit: www.shoeboxblog.com; used with permission.

Lead to Nowhere

This year's annual study of lead response behavior conducted by InsideSales.com on 696 companies with online lead forms revealed that sales reps were, on average, attempting their first call to a newly submitted web lead after 39 hours had passed.

Another alarming piece of data: nearly 36% of those audited *never* responded to a submitted lead during the entire two-week tracking period.[1]

---

[1] "The Great Marketing/Sales Disconnect: Industry Study Reveals 36% of Leads Never Called," Jan Johnson, Forbes.com, July 27, 2012, http://bit.ly/UnLeads.

Never, Ever

Fellas, listen closely to me.

Never, ever assume she's pregnant.

Unless she tells you to your face or you can see the head . . .

Pin the Tail on the Jackasses

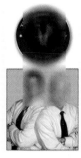

📌 Repin   ♥ Like   From

Howard County MD Real Estate Howard County MD Real Estate Find My Dream Home, Howard County MD Real Estate What's My Home Worth?, Howard County MD Real Estate Share/Save /Bookmark, Howard County MD Real Estate Welcome to Howard County Maryland, a burgeoning area centrally located between Baltimore and Washington, D.C. Howard County MD real estate options include properties in both Columbia and Ellicott City. Columbia was the first and most successful "planned community" in existence, and the Columbia-Ellicott City area was 4th on Money magazine's "America's Best Places to Live" list. The award-winning school system often ranks first in the state when comparing standardized data, and, as an added bonus, the U.S. Census Bureau cited the county as the third wealthiest in the nation when comparing median household incomes. The area is filled with history, charm, culture and economic vibrancy. You've chosen a prime area in which to make a real estate invest investment.   /ho...

Pinned via pinmarklet

Pinterest did not become popular by real estate agents pinning their brand identity photos.

And these guys took the asshattery further by outsourcing likes and repins so their faces could trend.

Some realtors hurt my soul.

Please Prove Your Business Is a Moron

Please prove you're not a robot

The mental powers of David Blaine, Sylvia Brown, and Kreskin couldn't decipher this captcha.

Not So Special

Linked in ® Account Type: Basic | Upgrade

Home   Profile   Contacts   Groups   **Jobs**   Inbox   Companies

ℹ Special offer: 0% off a 30 day job post.

Build your job posting

🏢 Work Environment

Frequently Futile

People always ask, "What is the best frequency to send out a newsletter?"

The best time to send out a newsletter is when you have something of value to share. If you offer no value, people will stop reading.

There are three reactions to an e-mail; read now, read later, or delete. "Will read later" is Latin for, "not reading later, see it three months from now, feel guilty, delete, and pretend I never got it."

Aim for the first category.

Friendly Fire

I once had someone call my office to ask why I had unfriended him on Facebook.

The very nature of him calling should have answered his question.

We Can Change

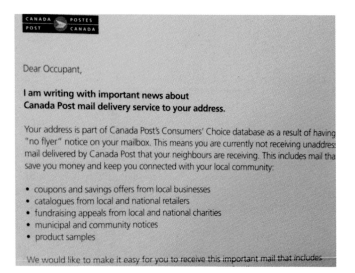

CANADA POST / POSTES CANADA

Dear Occupant,

I am writing with important news about Canada Post mail delivery service to your address.

Your address is part of Canada Post's Consumers' Choice database as a result of having "no flyer" notice on your mailbox. This means you are currently not receiving unaddres mail delivered by Canada Post that your neighbours are receiving. This includes mail tha save you money and keep you connected with your local community:

- coupons and savings offers from local businesses
- catalogues from local and national retailers
- fundraising appeals from local and national charities
- municipal and community notices
- product samples

We would like to make it easy for you to receive this important mail that includes

It sounds like I broke up with Canada Post.

Views Expressed

> **@reiver @neyugn Truth is, @unmarketing cannot fathom social media beyond his own utility, so his advice should be taken with a grain of salt**
>
> Aug 21, 2012 12:47p, from HootSuite
>
> **Bio:** Ambassador of Happiness at ▓▓▓▓. Yes, that's my job title. Views expressed are my own, not my company's.

"Views expressed are my own" is the most dangerous statement in social media.

Your people are your brand. And everything they say or share can and will affect your business.

For an Ambassador of Happiness, this guy didn't seem too jolly.

e-Moms

There are two kinds of people you do not want to piss off: geeks and moms.

And, if she is a geek mom . . .

Run.

The Fashionable Riot

Kenneth needs to learn that not all news is worth profiting from.

Golden Product Placement

"I have a great idea for an ad!"

"I have buses, billboards, tea cozies, and news-papers! What else could you possibly have thought of?"

"Urinals!"

" . . . that's GOLD! A Captive Audience!"

Figure Credit: Thanks to Julien Smith for sharing this one; used with permission.

Customer Disservice

Customer Service

| INSTANT ANSWERS | EMAIL US | CHAT | MY STUFF |

Chat with a Support Agent

* First Name:	
* Last Name:	
* Email Address:	
* Please Choose a Product:	▼
* Title:	-- ▼
* Address 1:	
Address 2:	
* City:	
* State/Province:	-- ▼
* Zip Code/Postal Code:	
* Country:	-- ▼
Phone :	

Enter your phone number in the following format: 111-111-1111
* Denotes a required field.
Submit Request

Thank goodness phone number is optional!

Everything else is apparently required for an online chat.

A Kitten Dies . . .

. . . any time someone tweets about their Klout/Kred score.

Influence is organic and subjective.

Get Off at the Next Stop

View emergency room wait times.
Because you just rear-ended a bus!

Don't Phone in Manners

For the 30 seconds it takes to place your order for coffee or pay your bill, put down your phone. Please.

Can't UnLink

It would be easier to return used underwear than to remove a LinkedIn connection.

Face Palm

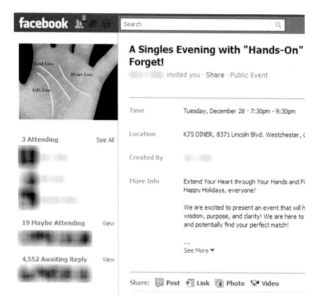

Ignoring the fact that this is a singles event with a picture of a palm . . .

If you look at the number of people awaiting reply versus those attending, you can see how we've broken Facebook events.

If you don't target geographically and demographically, don't use Facebook events.

Go Home Phone; You're Drunk

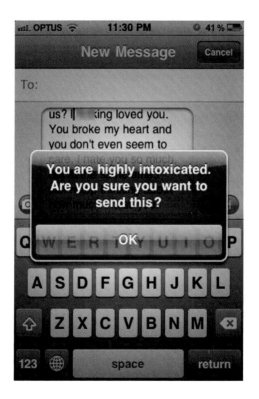

Nothing good comes out of your phone after 8 PM.

Self-Hatred

Looks like the National Association of Telemarketers isn't interested in any soliciting.

They don't even like themselves.

A Kitten Dies . . .

. . . when a guy posted on my speaking promo video that I needed to dress more appropriately for business.

When I went to check out his profile, I could see he had publically liked seven porn sites.

And I'm the inappropriate one.

Social Slam

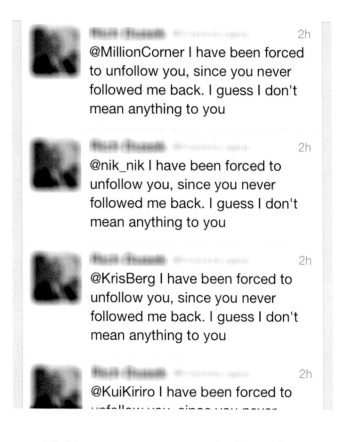

2h

@MillionCorner I have been forced to unfollow you, since you never followed me back. I guess I don't mean anything to you

2h

@nik_nik I have been forced to unfollow you, since you never followed me back. I guess I don't mean anything to you

2h

@KrisBerg I have been forced to unfollow you, since you never followed me back. I guess I don't mean anything to you

2h

@KuiKiriro I have been forced to unfollow you, since you never

Nothing says engagement quite like guilt.

Seems Legit

(SUSPECTED SPAM) MSN Update

mystery.shopperinc@live.com
Sent: Mon 27/08/2012 4:49 PM
To: Scott's e-mail

Hello,

Your e-mail will be closed if you don't reply with the below

Name:

SSN:

DOB:

Mother's Maiden Name:

E-mail:

Bank Name:

Reply Promptly,

E-mail Update Team

*   *   *

This is really more of an IQ test.

The End of Twitter

Schedule Tweets
Set up your Twitter updates to be
sent at the time you want.
Learn more

Auto Follow
Automatically follow new followers,
optionally send a welcome DM.
Learn more

Unfollow your non-followers
Quickly and easily unfollow the
Twitter users not following you.
Learn more

If there were three horsemen of social media, there they are. And this product offers you all three!

You don't have to be present. You don't have to choose whom to follow.

And as a bonus, it will unfollow anyone who isn't engaging (kind of like you).

This is going to be the end of Twitter.

All Your Privacy Belongs to Us

In December 2012, Randi Zuckerberg tweeted, complaining about someone sharing her private family photos online.

Randi Zuckerberg . . . the sister of the guy who owns and sells all of our information on Facebook, a website known for their ever-changing, confusing privacy settings.

Let's just say her Twitter complaints were not met with a lot of support.

Too Much Transparency

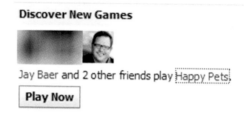

I still can't look Jay in the eye.[2]

---

[2] Happy Pets is one of many social games played on Facebook. If you don't play, I'd like to be your friend.

A Social Layer

Google+ user numbers are calculated by how many people use their Google account in the year. Google claims the social site is a layer, or portal, part of the site.

So any time you use YouTube, Google search, Gmail, Calendar—or heck any website/service that is part of the Google empire that you've logged into Google with—it counts as a use of Google+.

Oh, and for anyone who has signed up for a new Gmail account since Google+ launched? That counts as a Google+ login, too, even if you never set up a profile on Google+.

Long Presentation Slide

A Kitten Has Died During Your Presentation If...

- Everything you say is on the screen
- You need two hands to count the number of bullet points on a slide
- You bring in all your bullet points at once and pretend people don't read ahead
- You use Comic Sans as your slide font because it's fun
- You use animation for fonts or slide transitions
- You use sound effects to bring in each point
- Showed up with a Mac and no dongle for the projector
- You think the talk is about you.

A Kitten Dies . . .

. . . whenever you say the two worst words to a customer looking for help with a problem: "It's policy."

Exiting Your Brand

I was waiting for the third pop-up offering to pay me a dollar to take their product.

A Kitten Dies . . .

". . . if you post your own quote on social media, or in your e-mail signature, complete with your name after."

—*Scott Stratten*

Fighting Foodies

At Least They Cleaned the Important Part

The amount of QR codes on trucks has reached an epidemic point. Look here: we have a freshly applied one spotted in the wild. Do truckers walk around lots scanning each other's trailers?

Vote for the Most Annoying Person

Most voting contests are created to leverage your friends to increase website traffic.

Only the website wins.

And truly we all lose from the endless begging for votes.

Looks Like Magazines Do Still Have ROI

Susan,

We recently published an interview with you in our February 4 issue. I found your article very interesting and informative. Then looked at your website and I was overwhelmed with all you have going on. Congratulations!

I wanted to let you know about our reprint service. It's a great way to extend the value of that publicity.

For a small fee, your article will be professionally reprinted and a logo may be added. You can use article reprints for marketing, promotional material, trade shows, sales kits and press kits.

For only $295 we will produce a pdf-formatted reprint. You can then make unlimited hard copies and post it on your website or use it for other promotional purposes.

Turnaround time is usually around two weeks. We will invoice you upon completion.

Attached is a sample of a recent reprint that we did for another company that was profiled in the Daily Herald Business Ledger.

Please let me know if you would like to take advantage of this opportunity.

Best regards,

*   *   *

I'm not sure which is worse: charging someone for taking a clipping of his or her own article or the fact that it's going to take the company two weeks to create a PDF.

Drive-by Articles

The saving grace of LinkedIn is the group functionality. The ability to share discussions with industry peers or ones of like minds is incredible. Sadly, running one of these groups is a daily battle at removing drive-by spam disguised as articles. You know the ones; the person posts, "Thought this would be interesting!" or "Hope this generates discussion!" and then posts the article in 10 groups, where it's a bunch of regurgitated drivel designed for you to check out that person's blog or read his or her profile. Want to start a discussion? Post a question and want answers that are not your own. No one asked you.

CHAPTER 3

They're Selfish

It's a Bird! It's a Plane!

No, it's a QR code being pulled by an airplane . . .

Admit it; you just want to have a QR code. You can't even help yourself.

They're shiny and new. They show that you and your business are on the cutting edge of tech.

Experts are telling you that you need to have one.

The thing is, we need to be doing things in business because we should, not only because we can.

QR codes are selfish. Just look at this QR code being pulled behind a plane. Seriously? How selfish can you really be? I know one of you reading this approved the budget for it.

You know what makes them really easy to show off? A plane and the wide-open sky.

You know what makes scanning a code really difficult? Motion and distance.

In this section, we are going to look at all the selfish things we do in business. From trying to control customer feedback to ignoring customers altogether, these examples are all about us.

Nobody Cares about Your Logo

No one ever ate at your crappy restaurant and said, "The food was cold, the service was bad, but *did you see the logo*?! It's exquisite. We have to come back next Thursday!"

Checking Out

74% of Americans are unfamiliar with the concept of checking in to a location via mobile device, and only 3% have ever checked in. Even more damning, is that 4% had checked in when surveyed in 2011. This is a 25% decrease in check in behaviors in a single year. It's not going to rebound, which is why Foursquare's play is to be the new Yelp.[1]

—Jay Baer

---

[1] Jay Baer (convicted Happy Pets player from earlier), "11 Shocking New Social Media Statistics in America," *The Social Habit* (blog), Convince & Convert, accessed June 3, 2013, www.convinceand convert.com/the-social-habit/11-shocking-new-social-media-statistics-in-america/.

Tell Me What to Say

7,140 like this

👍 **Like**

2 hours ago · 🔗

Dear Facebook fans,

Please only post positive comments on our page. Any negative comments will be removed. If you have a problem with your membership or complaints about any of the facilities you must call our Member Experience Department at: 1–800– ▓▓ ▓▓

I know what they are trying to say, but wording is everything. What they should have said was, "We appreciate your feedback and encourage anyone who has an issue with one of our clubs to call us so that we can take care of your issue immediately and directly, because many issues can involve confidential information."

Not the Time

After any sort of tragedy, a brand should do one of two things: be quiet or offer support. Notice a choice is not, "Try to leverage the tragedy into website traffic."

Camera Shy

Photo Not Available

This could have been a picture of your new product tweeted out to more than 100,000 followers. But you stopped me from taking a picture in your store and said "No pictures. It's policy."

Well played?

It Can Hurt to Ask

From: <removed>
Sent: Mar 25, 2013 8:39AM

Hey Scott! We've talked a few times before and you've always helped me out. Can you take a look at my new website? <**URL removed**>

*   *   *

Nothing says thanks quite like asking for more free advice.

Simply Selfish

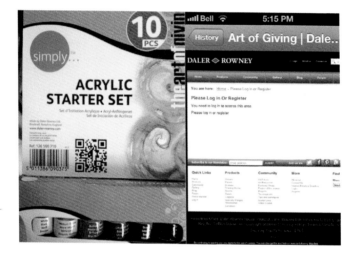

My son asked me to scan his paint set. The result is on the right. You can mess with me, marketers, but now you're messing with my kid.

Children Are Our Future

 Rattlesden School
RattlesdenPS

Our twitter account does not want conversations or interactions with individuals or groups outside our own community or other schools.

3:36pm - 9 Dec 12

> What do we want? Conversation!
> Where do we want it? STOP TALKING!

It's Still Burning

shared KJCTNews8's photo.

Friends, this is why we have insurance. I know it's not fun to pay premiums (kind of like taxes) but we at
                        Insurance are here for you and your family in the event of some terrible loss. I would be honored to insure you, your families and friends. If you have any insurance related questions. Please let me know. :)

| Multiple homes destroyed in Dotsero blaze...

If you're going to try and profit from a local fire, at least wait until it's been put out.

Actually, just don't do it at all.

If Pinocchio Had Teeth

Well, at least someone likes them.

Are We Dating?

We Miss You!

We noticed you haven't responded to our emails. Currently you receive personalized recommendations, offers and information about in-store events. If you would like to continue receiving emails from us, **click here**.

If you do not respond, you will no longer receive emails from us.

This reminds me of a girlfriend I had in high school.

It's okay to check in with your customers to see if they're getting value from your newsletter. But threatening to break up with them is a little much.

Gimme Some More

⌷ Subscribe by Email

The only ***required field** is your email address, but I'd like to get to know you better.

* indicates required

First Name

Last Name

Title

Company

Email Address *

Twitter

To send someone a newsletter, the only thing you need is that person's e-mail address.

I know why companies want all this information, but why should people want to give it to you?

Every field you request after e-mail address reduces your conversions.

Fashion for Who?

Your PR campaign falling flat is not a social media problem.

Looking for someone to promote your new line of women's athletic gear? You may have the wrong person.

And when someone says no thanks, remember to stop trying. It's not anyone's job to delete your bad PR emails. It is your job not to send them.

Sub QR

Figure Credit: www.marketoonist.com; used with permission.

e-Service Extraordinaire

Technology can make customer service more efficient, scalable, and responsive than ever before.

Or, it can just make it as miserable as usual.

Figure Credit: Thanks to Consumerist.com; used with permission.

Maybe Their Phone Camera Is Detachable

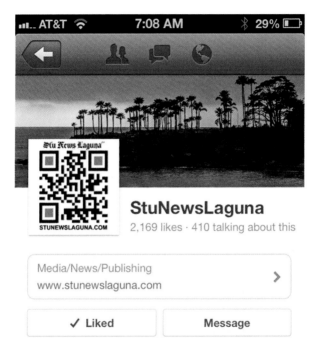

A QR code as its profile pic on its Facebook page, as seen through a mobile phone. Read that sentence as many times as it takes to make you realize the absurdity.

A Million Reasons to Cry

1 Million Twitter and 1 Million Facebook Followers
Elance - Toronto, ON
See original job posting at Elance »

Hello I am looking for a followers for both my twitter account and my facebook account * I have no
preference about where the followers come from we just need the numbers. * I will NOT provide you
with any passwords, sorry Desired Skills: SEM, Social Media Marketing
Elance - 1 day ago - save job - block

» View or apply to job

Everything that is wrong with social media
explained in one job posting.

A Kitten Dies . . .

. . . every time someone takes your business card at an event and uses it to sign you up for his or her newsletter. Stop it.

The Big #Truth

 Geoffrey Miller
@matingmind **1**

Dear obese PhD applicants: if you didn't have the willpower to stop eating carbs, you won't have the willpower to do a dissertation #truth

6/2/13 12:23 PM

 Geoffrey Miller
@matingmind **2**

Obviously my previous tweet does not represent the selection policies of any university, or my own selection criteria.

2013-06-02 8:20 PM

 Geoffrey Miller
@matingmind **3**

My sincere apologies to all for that idiotic, impulsive, and badly judged tweet. It does not reflect my true views, values, or standards.

2013-06-02 8:21 PM

4

@matingmind's tweets are protected.
Only confirmed followers have access to @matingmind's complete profile. Click the "Follow" button to send a follo

Here we see the four stages of a horrible apology. For an even more horrible tweet.

Finally getting to stage four, where he takes a new route, of the scapegoat, and says it was "for research"![2]

---

[2] To read more about this check out my post about it here: http://www.unmarketing.com/2013/06/06/why-tweets-about-obese-doctors-are-never-your-own/.

Perspective Is Everything

This is the real estate version of a bad avatar or online dating pic.

I'm Not Saying T-Mobile Is Terrible at Twitter, But . . .

Jessica Northey
@JessicaNorthey

Following ▾

NOTE that even if @TMobile service doesn't work for you AFTER you purchase it they will NOT waive Early Termination Fee. cc @TMobileHelp

← Reply ⇄ Retweet ★ Favorite

T-Mobile USA
@TMobileHelp

Follow ▾

@jessicanorthey We're sorry it didn't work for you.Not to sound rude, but after the buyers remorse then you're under contract. ^AS

If you are ever going to start off a sentence with, "Not to sound rude, but . . . ," don't say it.

It's like saying, "I'm not saying you're ugly, but . . ."

I would also say they might have been more careful with their words, considering Jessica had gone all caps thrice.

Nothing Says Social Like SHOUTING

LinkedIn

Lizzie Chen has sent you a message.

Date: 3/18/2013

Subject: WE ARE SOCIAL

WE ARE SOCIAL:
Facebook: https://www.facebook.com/dinowillfan
Twitter: https://twitter.com/DinowillFan
YouTube: https://www.youtube.com/
    DinowillFan
Google+: https://plus.google.com/u/0/
    100686063147490096329/posts
VK[3]: http://vk.com/dinowill
Blog: http://blog.dinowill.com

*   *   *

Your LinkedIn contact Lizzie would like you to know that THEY ARE SOCIAL.

---

[3] www.VK.com is a European social networking website.

I'm Pretty Sure This Is . . .

Entrapment.

Figure Credit: Thanks to @the_r33c3 for sharing; used with permission.

Gap in Judgment

GAP BE BRIGHT

Gap ✔
@Gap

🐦 **Follow**

All impacted by #Sandy, stay safe! We'll be doing lots of Gap.com shopping today. How about you? 4sq.com/QPVDT9

← Reply 🔁 Retweet ⭐ Favorite

A check-in at Frankenstorm Apocalypse - Hurricane Sandy

Other Great Outdoors in New York, NY

✉ **Foursquare** @foursquare · Follow

This tweet should have ended after the first sentence.

The Most Misleading Man in the World

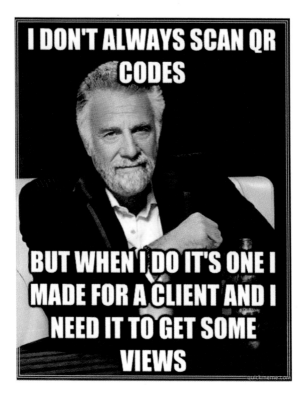

Opt Out/In

Spammers confirm your e-mail when you ask to opt out, making it even more valuable.

Number One

Real-time results for **toronto plane crash**   ⊕ Save this search

1 new tweet since you started searching.

VirginAmerica #HeartCanada Toronto is our 1st Intl dest &
w/ WiFi, food on-demand & more you'll fly in style. Starting
6.23.10: http://bit.ly/VX2Toronto
24 minutes ago via web
Promoted by Virgin America   ⇄ 2 Retweets   ↱ Reply ⇄ Retweet

TrafficServices 4 seater **plane crash** is in Markham, not
Toronto. Emergency crews from York Region are responding.
3 minutes ago via TweetDeck
⇄ 2 Retweets

robpatrob **plane crash** in **toronto** - antone know anything?
2 minutes ago via TweetDeck
⇄ 1 Retweet

Ranking number one in all searches isn't always
best.

Twitter Is Not a Megaphone

Twitter is a terrible broadcast tool. It's a conversation, not a dictation.

A Kitten Dies . . .

. . . whenever a company promotes from within, without basing it on merit.

Employees who are awesome and doing their best for customers and the company should be rewarded.

Can You Hear Me Now?

Nothing says, "We want your business," like the kiosk circle of shun (all four are employees).

It's a Trap

When choosing a background, be sure to view it on all monitor sizes, not just your own.

You Are the Weakest Link

If you request to connect with me on LinkedIn and the first thing you do is pitch your business, you're doing relationships wrong.

The whole point of a connection is to connect first.

Don't Trend

You should do a little research into why a term is trending before trying to profit from it.

Aurora, Colorado, was the site of a 2012 shooting during the midnight screening of *The Dark Knight Rises*.

You Get What You Pay For

fiverr®

I will create a video testimony positively reviewing your business, website, or product for $5

People will look for shortcuts.

Is it really too much to make a great product, or provide a valued service, instead of paying for reviews?

Score!

I'll let you pull out the calculator on this one.

The Direct Mail Merge Tweet

Yellowstone Capital
@YSCapital

Follow

<< Test First Name >> You have been
Pre-Approved for A Line of Credit for your
Business *|MMERGE3|* - eepurl.com
/ovGR1

← Reply   ⇄ Retweet   ★ Favorite

This tweet alone killed four kittens and my soul.

The iQRony

BrandManageCamp.com

Figure Credit: www.BrandManageCamp.com; used with permission.

Automated Authenticity

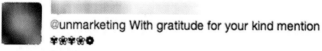

@unmarketing With gratitude for your kind mention ✿❀✿❀●

Details

She auto-thanked me for my tweet questioning the validity of her best-selling book about Twitter.

Read that again.

The QR Matrix

Image: Brad Friedman

author of two other books of his I've read; The End Of Business As Usual and Engage. It's a hard-bound, square-shaped, coffee table like book filled with some incredibly creative "Visualization" by Hugh MacLeod and his team at Social Object Factory. Continue reading →

Use Your Smartphone To Scan & Find Us On The Web

[Search]

Recommend 13 people recommend this. Be the first of your friends.

Posted in General Business Advice, Social Media | Tagged Brian Solis, Business, Digital Strategy, postaweek2013, Tips, WTF | 2 Comments

Tags
brands Business Communication Digital Strategy Facebook Google Information Flow LinkedIn Marketing postaweek2011 postaweek2012 postaweek2013 Privacy Sharing Social Media Social Media Marketing Social Networks Social Networks Technology Tips Tools Twitter

The Friedman Group Is Named 2012 Constant Contact All Star

Posted on March 30, 2013 by Brad Friedman

The Friedman Group, LLC, a business working with professionals and businesses to enhance their online image and take advantage of the power of inbound and social media marketing, has received the 2012 All Star Award from Constant Contact®, Inc., the trusted marketing adviser to more than half a million small organizations worldwide. Each year, a select group of Constant Contact customers are honored with the All Star Award for their exemplary marketing results. The Friedman Group, LLC's results ranked among the top 10% of Constant Contact's customer base **for the second year in a row.** Continue reading →

Categories
[Select Category]

Recent Comments
- Brad Friedman on Review: Brian Solis' 'What's The Future Of

Ya know where the QR code takes me when I scan it?

Back to the website!

Antisocial Behavior Is the New Social Media

Red Medicine @redmedicinela   23 Mar
All the nice guests who wonder why restaurants overbook and they
sometimes have to wait for their res should thank people like those
below.
Expand

Red Medicine @redmedicinela   23 Mar
Also, big thanks to Carlos ▉▉▉, Colin ▉▉, Allison ▉▉▉,
Sam ▉▉, Daniella ▉▉▉, and Matt ▉▉▉ for no-showing btwn
730p-930p.
Expand

Red Medicine @redmedicinela   23 Mar
Hi Kyle ▉▉▉ (323), I hope you enjoyed your gf's bday and the
flowers that you didn't bring when you no-showed for your 815 res.
Thanks.
Expand ← Reply ⇄ Retweet ★ Favorite ••• More

I'm a fan of naming and shaming, but this even
gave me the creeps.

Drawing a Blank

It took me a long time to decide whether I wanted to see the blank pop-up again.

Wait until You See It . . .

Look closely.
There you go.

Your Time Is Better Spent Elsewhere

When I speak to audiences around the world about QR codes, I almost always find their defenders. I am told about amazing marketing campaigns, creative possibilities, and practical applications (usually from QR code designers . . .)

> QR can change the way we use our mobile phones, Scott!
>
> QR codes will connect mobile users to companies like never before, Scott!
>
> Look at all the cool ways they are being used around the world, Scott!

The best examples are usually in retail applications. And I must admit, some of them are pretty amazing.

The grocery chain Tesco has virtual shopping stores where codes are used to scan items, which are then delivered to you. I love the idea of shopping this way. How great to be able to scan some milk and bread on your way to work in the morning and have it show up on your way home.

The codes worked, and the shoppers used them. QR codes at their best.

The thing is, like with all new technologies and applications, if your business is already in trouble, adding them will not make it better. If your product or service sucks, using social media or focusing valuable energy on new technology like QR codes will not fix your issues. They will simply amplify them.

In January 2013, while in the middle of a horse-meat scandal, the Twitter account for Tesco tweeted the following:

If you're in the middle of a huge meat scandal, maybe lay off the word *hay* in your tweets.

No cool QR code application is going to take back that mistake.

If you don't have the time or resources to manage your social media accounts properly, or your product quality control for that matter, you shouldn't be focusing on new technologies. Your time is better spent elsewhere.

In this section we are going to look at something you need to be doing, or not doing, before looking at QR codes and other bright, shiny technologies.

Always Pay Your Web Designer

DEAR FITNESS SF CUSTOMER,

FITNESS SF preferred to ignore our invoices instead of paying them. As a result this website is no longer operational.

We regret any inconvenience this may cause for you as a customer of Fitness SF, however it is a necessary measure in getting what is rightfully ours.

Half a year's worth of work, including GALLERY FEATURED logo renderings with OVER 1,300 VIEWS a piece.

While some of that got replaced in an attempt to cover up our work, other parts, like the base design (CSS) of the site were still used, illegally as they've not been paid for.

Normally there is no question of paying one's dues. It is simply a matter of morals. Having morals and acting upon them or not having any and just betraying the people that got you started. Sadly we've come to know what Fitness SF stands for, or you wouldn't be reading this.

Your word on their Facebook accounts will go a long way. We're a small company in the heart of Europe, which is probably why Fitness SF believes they can sit this out till we perish. Can you support a company that acts like this?

View more of our work for Fitness SF on ADWEEK | BEHANCE

I'm sure they'll work it out.
See what I did there?

Who Are They Talking To?

 Elixir Bistro Galt (@ElixirGalt)
yes better you do not come with you screaming brat and scare my regular customars

Sat Apr 23 03:51:35 2011

Can you find the five errors in this tweet?

Consider Location

Supply chain management.
You're doing it right.[1]

---

[1] Credit to my kids, who spotted this. They demand recognition.
Aidan and Owen, please withdraw your lawsuit now.

Value Good Employees

I'm assuming this is a seasonal award.

Figure Credit: Thanks for sharing @ricksmithjr; used with permission.

Just Say No to Scheduling

Sometimes U have to Blow things up in order to see clearly #Leadership

is that the BEST choice of words?
Details   16m

I Yeah, that was scheduled and not reviewed. Epic fail on my part   1m

This tweet was sent soon after the Boston Marathon bombings. Whatever minuscule artificial gain you get from scheduling your terrible motivational quotes will never equal the repercussions of a tweet like this.

Invest in Communication Training

City of Vaughan
@City_of_Vaughan

Everyone on my street has double
gararges...who are these cknuts
who don't put their car in the
garage when we get 2 feet of snow?
#dumb

2013-02-08 7:23 AM

41 RETWEETS **11** FAVORITES

That's one way to talk about your citizens.

Don't Be an Asshole

KitchenAid
@KitchenAidUSA

Obamas gma even knew it was
going 2 b bad! 'She died 3 days b4
he became president'. #nbcpolitics

The views expressed are not those of my blender.

Remember to Switch to Your Personal Account

I find it ironic that Detroit is known as the #motorcity and yet no one here knows how to ██cking drive

about 3 hours ago via web   ← Reply ♈ Re

ChryslerAutos
Chrysler Autos

Even Eminem thinks this is offensive.

A Message to Fast Food Workers

Let's be honest, who hasn't licked a stack of tacos?

The difference is, when I was young, we didn't have cameras in our phones. Or Facebook. Or Twitter.

Maybe lick them in private.

Remember, Not Everything Is a Marketing Opportunity

9 hours ago · Like

Share my page
Photography and help me 2 gain more clients ...I Will donate 15%
of my gross income to the families Sandy Hook Elementary Victims !
thank u ....I want to help
9 hours ago · Like · 👍 4

really????
2 hours ago · Like · 👍 7

You should just donate the 15%...why do people
always want something out of a tragedy???
about an hour ago · Like · 👍 44

Exactally , let these poor families mourn
without trying to make money on them .leave the families alone ,
about an hour ago · Like · 👍 28

Disgusting Heather!
58 minutes ago · Like · 👍 22

Heather this is not the time or place. This is not
how you help.
49 minutes ago · Like · 👍 10

@Heather you are a horrible person, if you
want to help, just fucking help. And promote your shit somewhere
else. 20 children and six heroes are dead or did you not watch the
news??
46 minutes ago · Like · 👍 18

A train wreck of conditional giving.

Remember, People Are Listening

Raúl R. Labrador (R) @Raul_Labrador

Me likey Broke Girls.

Deleted 3 months ago after 14 seconds, originally posted via Twitter for iPhone

reply

retweet

Me likey politicians who tweet without context.

At Least Her First Name Isn't Richard

First name	Emily
Last name	Dick
	You used a bad word: Dick. Please clean up the language and try again.
Signature ⓘ	
Title	Sr. Specialist, Global Marketing Operations
Company	Epicor Software Corporation
Location	Vancouver, BC

Isn't it bad enough she's had to deal with people making fun of her last name, without problems like this one?

Figure Credit: Emily Dick; used with permission.

Don't Get Caught Flying the Bird

This job would be so much easier without all these pesky people on the plane (a flight attendant took this picture. Sorry . . . I mean an ex-flight attendant took this picture).

A Kitten Dies . . .

. . . every time you have a meeting about meetings.

Remember, Youth Is Wasted on the Young

Someone needs to assassinate
Obama...like ASAP
#DieYouPieceOfSl_t

Secret Service investigates 16-year-old Alyssa Douglas' tweet about assassinating President Obama

1:24 PM, Sep 7, 2012 | comments

(Cincinnati.com) -- Alyssa Douglas, a high school girl from the Clarksville area of Ohio, sent out a tweet Thursday night saying: "Someone needs to assassinate Obama...like ASAP #DieYouPieceOfS__ "

This was dumb, even from a teenager's perspective. At 140 characters, that's still a death threat.

Don't Drive Your Customers to the Brink

Twitter didn't invent complaining about bad products or service.

A Kitten Dies . . .

. . . every time we value swag more than people.

The president of a company who had recently experienced a lot of layoffs once told me, with a straight face, that he couldn't understand why no one was excited about the 10,000 golf balls they'd just ordered with their logo on them.

Leave the swag to Jay-Z.

All-Caps Ketchup

Do you feel bad for the person who did this or the one who has to clean it up?

If you say the second, remember that whoever did this had the time and the privacy to go all-caps ketchup!

And underline in mustard.

You Could Stand to Lose a Few Teeth

If you plan on insulting a waitress, plan on being hunted down by the Internet. Reddit users hunted the man down. Sadly, it ended up being the wrong guy, with the same name.

Remember, Sometimes Private Messages, Go Public

Remember when you used to pass love notes in class? This is like passing a billboard.

Figure Credit: Thanks to @kylehillman for sharing; used with permission.

Don't Hire Idiot Employees

 PabstCanada 3h
Rule #1 at Club
Tropicana @**trashkill**
@**a_crooks** instagr.am/
p/OSeyvUBbPa/

I can't say this enough: Tweeting a picture, retweeting something, or quoting implies endorsement unless otherwise noted. No fat chicks? Really?

The Peak of Creative Stupidity

If you're going to fondle the mashed potato boob you just created, for the love of gravy, don't take a picture and share it online.

(Yes, she was fired.)

A Kitten Dies . . .

. . . every time someone has to spend 38 weeks on a committee making decisions about brochure fonts. You know who should design things? Designers.

I Can't Breathe, I'm Laughing So Hard

Hi

I found your ad at the Career Center the other day. I was wondering if the position was still available and if you could give me some more information about it. I've attached my resume and cover letter for your consideration.

Regards,

8765i.jpg
33K View Download

~~JESUS CHRIST~~ I ACCIDENTALLY SENT MY POTENTIAL FUTURE BOSS A PICTURE OF NIC CAGE RATHER THAN MY COVER LETTER+RESUME, WHICH WAS A ZIP FILE TITLED WITH A BUNCH OF NUMBERS LIKE THE JPG I ACCIDENTALLY ATTACHED OH MY GOD

This wins. At e-mail and everything else.

Stop Scheduling Tweets

 CBC News Alerts
@CBCAlerts   🐦 Follow   👤▾

1 dead in stage collapse prior to Radiohead
Toronto show . 3 others hurt, says Toronto
EMS. #radiohead

 **Live Nation Ontario**
@LiveNationON   🐦 Follow   👤▾

Help us create a @radiohead photo album
from the show! Share your Instagram
photos from the show tonight with the
hashtag #RadioheadTO

↩ Reply   ↨ Retweet   ★ Favorite

58 **Corey Herscu** @cellguru   17m
well done managing your pre-scheduled tweets
@LiveNationON
Details

47 **Jason Hudson** @_JasonHudson   25m
PR 101: Cancel your scheduled-Tweets. RT
@LiveNationON Help create @radiohead album! Share
photos from the show w/ the hashtag #RadioheadTO

 27 **Ryan Allen** @allen_26er   20m
@LiveNationON are you guys ▩▩ing stupid? Here's
your photo you thoughtless ▩▩ks.
pic.twitter.com/9UKZtAwx

This concert was cancelled due to a stage collapse
that killed a drum tech.

Opinions Are Your Brand's Reflection

You have the right to your opinion.
Your employer has the right to fire you.

Less Than Joyful

 Joy Haven
15 hours ago near Dickinson, ND ·

I am so sick of old people It is to loud Why do they bitch when they will be gone before they know it. Maybe because they know they spent their whole life for the wrong purpose. Themselves. Who cares about them. It is about others. May they rest in piece when the day comes.

I'm in the Middle of an Awkward Sandwich

#awkward
#ThatsHisBoss

Not So Friendly

Wait until you see it.

For all of us that have worked tables, and for all of us parents that have taken children out for dinner, we have thought this.

We just never left this kind of evidence.

We Want "Whatever Your Name Is" Back!

 **Amber Naslund**
6 minutes ago

Classic. Had the same insurance with Allstate for six plus years, never heard a peep from my agent. Never.

I switch to State Farm. Allstate agent gets the cancellation and emails me, lamenting that I "didn't give him a chance to review my needs first."

Uh. Dude. Loyalty is earned when you do something to earn it. You had SIX YEARS.

I bet the agent was excited about the company rolling out QR codes last year. Eyes on the prize, people.

Happy clients = Loyal clients.

Take Away the Virtual Keys after Firing Someone

If you're going to fire the person who runs your company's Twitter account, you should make sure that person isn't live tweeting it.

A Kitten Dies . . .

. . . WHEN YOU USE ALL CAPS IN AN
E-MAIL/TEXT/TWEET OR POST.
   WE THINK YOU'RE YELLING AT US.
   Stop it.

Don't Fake an Ovation

I once saw a speaker who claimed to get a standing ovation every time he spoke.

In reality, at the end of the talk, he asked every one to stand up and stretch. So they were already standing when he wrapped up.

The English Swear the Best

OMG I HATE MY JOB!! My boss is a total pervvy wanker always making me do ▇it stuff just to piss me off!! WANKER!
Yesterday at 18:03 · Comment · Like

Hi ▇, i guess you forgot about adding me on here?
Firstly, don't flatter yourself. Secondly, you've worked here 5 months and didn't work out that i'm gay? I know i don't prance around the office like a queen, but it's not exactly a secret. Thirdly, that '▇it stuff is called your 'job', you know, what i pay you to do. But the fact that you seem able to ▇ck-up the simplest of tasks might contribute to how you feel about it. And lastly, you also seem to have forgotten that you have 2 weeks left on your 6 month trial period. Don't bother coming in tomorrow. I'll pop your P45 in the post, and you can come in whenever you like to pick up any stuff you've left here. And yes, i'm serious.
Yesterday at 22:53

Write a comment...

The first rule of Facebook: your boss will always see your updates, one way or another.

Wheel of Misfortune

Jennifer Ditchburn @jenditchburn   18m
RT @TheBrazman: no wonder I didn't mention why with
the assinine reports you guys have to make. No regard
for personal lives or situations.
Details

SenPatrickBrazeau   🕊 Follow   👤▾
@TheBrazman

@jenditchburn while u smile Jen, others
suffer. Change the D to a B in your last name
and we're even! Don't mean it but needs
saying.

↩ Reply   🔁 Retweet   ★ Favorite

Like any four-year-old can tell you, name-calling
is never, ever a good idea.

That last sentence hurts my brain.

Remember Your Manners

No matter who you are.

No matter how much money you make or the kind of car your drive.

No matter how many followers or likes you get.

That doesn't excuse you from common courtesy.

Manners matter.

Psychic Opt Out

Unsubscribe

Your email is alison@nummies.com.

WAIT!

Are you leaving because of too many emails?

You can still receive valuable offers from FTD.com! Click the "one email per week" button below to change your frequency and receive these offers only once per week instead of unsubscribing.

ONE EMAIL PER WEEK

OR

Do you want to unsubscribe?

If you prefer not to receive discount email offers, simply click the "Unsubscribe" button

Please help us understand why you're leaving (click all that apply).

☐ I was not happy with your products or service.

☐ I prefer to use another company for my flowers & gifts.

☐ I was receiving too many emails each week.

☐ Your email was not valuable to me.

Other (please specify)

You have **500** characters left.

UNSUBSCRIBE

You know you send too many e-mails when you guess the problem beforehand.

A Kitten Dies . . .

. . . every time a speaker tells you to turn off your phone during his or her talk.

If the speaker you've hired, or the talk you're giving, isn't more interesting than Angry Birds, you have a problem unplugging won't solve.

It's the job of the person on stage to be so awesome, knowledgeable, and engaging that the audience wants to pay attention.

Pay Attention to Privacy

Twenty-five percent of Facebook users don't use any kind of privacy settings.[2]

What could possibly go wrong?

---

[2] "Social Media Statistics and Facts 2012 [Infographic]," *GO-Globe .com* (blog), October 30, 2012, www.go-globe.com/blog/social-media-facts/.

Hire Better Employees

 StubHub
@StubHub

Thank f k it's Friday! Can't wait to get out of this stubsucking hell hole.

Looks like someone stubbed a toe.

Never Forget

Outrage doesn't take the weekend off.

When it hits the fan in business, that is not the time to hide behind the fan. The faster you can reply to negative feedback, the better your chance of coming out better on the other side.

Figure Credit: Thanks to Chris Farias and @KiteString my amazing design team; used with permission.

Don't Invite Open-Ended Insults

Coles Supermarkets
@Coles

🕊 Follow 👤▾

Finish this sentence: In my house it's a crime not to buy _____

33 RETWEETS   **5** FAVORITES   m.k

8:25 PM - 6 Mar 12 via HootSuite · Embed this Tweet

↩ Reply   🔁 Retweet   ★ Favorite

Dr Buttocks @drbuttocks   14h
@Coles Didn't think that one through, did you? This is going to be hilarious.

DESTANY @Hushlittlebabyd   14h
@Coles not buy coles brand products because of the benifits of no added msg and no artificial colours

ExStaffer @ExStaffer   14h
@Coles fruit & veg from a place that pays their farmers fair prices & sells seasonal produce not stored in a freezer or artificially ripened

Be careful crowdsourcing a phrase.

When you ask an open-ended question, people will answer however they want.

And the answers you don't want often travel the farthest.

Conclusion

QR codes are a lot like me when I was a teenager.

My mom used to say that I had potential. At the time I just assumed she meant I was awesome.

Figure Credit: Matt Edwards, Image Creator; Fred Beecher, Photo; used with permission.

It wasn't until I was a parent that I really understood what she was saying.

Potential meant that right then, teenage me, sucked. But one day, she hoped, she'd be able to talk to the neighbors about me without mentioning the word *parole*.

QR codes are full of potential—when they work.

Just now, I saw seven QR codes in a magazine. Three led to error pages, three went to non-mobile-friendly pages, and one worked.

We can do better than this.

If websites worked only one out of every seven times we tried them, there would be nobody surfing the Internet.

If you answered your phone only one out of every seven times it rang, people would stop calling.

I say, take a mulligan on QR codes and start fresh. We need to ask ourselves if our market is ready for them. Are we ready for them? Is our website ready for them?

Until the answer to those questions is yes, we should focus on creating great products, great services, and great experiences.

If you have any examples of your own that you'd like to share, you can tweet them to me @unmarketing, tag them on Instagram #unmarketing, or e-mail them to me at scott@QRcodeskillkittens.com.

If you want to bring this message, along with what you should be doing in business, to your conference or company, drop us a line at Scott@un-marketing.com, call us at 888-580-9969, or drop by www.scottstratten .com to see me in action, read testimonials, and see session descriptions.

No kittens are harmed in any performances . . . but some brands are.